DANGER

HIGH VOLTAGE

Electrical Safety

We will take care
with electricity.

3

We will take care
with this electricity.

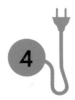

5

My dad will take care
with the electric iron.

My dad will take care
with the electric bulb.

9

My sister will take care
with the electric hairdryer.

11

My brother will take care
with the electric toaster.

We will all take care

in this storm.

15

We will stay inside.